The Observer launched the Great Green Limerick Competition in association with Friends of the Earth on 16 April 1989, the first Sunday of Environment Week. Each limerick was submitted with a £1 entry fee which was donated to Friends of the Earth.

The competition was divided into 3 categories – 5 to 11 years of age, 12 to 16, and 17 and over. Limericks were required to be on 'green' topics involving the environment, nature or conservation.

The judges were Jonathon Porritt, the director of Friends of the Earth, Geoffrey Lean, Environmental Correspondent of *The Observer*, and Katherine Whitehorn, also from *The Observer*.

Selected limericks from *The Observer* Great Green Limerick Competition run in association with Friends of the Earth

Great Green LIMERICKS

illustrated by Quentin Blake

published by
the Paperback Division of
W.H. Allen & Co. Plc

A Star Book
Published in 1989
by the Paperback Division of
W.H. Allen & Co. Plc
Sekforde House, 175/9 St. John
Street, London, EC1V 4LL

Printed in Great Britain by

ISBN 0 352 32658 1

Great Green LIMERICKS

FOREWORD

Given the whereabouts of the town of Limerick, it's somewhat surprising that we didn't receive a single offering about little green leprechauns at the bottom of the garden! Our authors would seem to be much more preoccupied with the ozone layer, the state of our beaches, and the contribution to the Greenhouse Effect with all that hot air from our politicians.

The joy of the limerick is its extraordinary diversity, matching all our moods, appealing to all our humours. It's actually none too easy to get people rolling in the aisles about the laying waste of life on Earth, and the anger and frustration that so many of us still feel at this criminal folly is well represented in this collection. Generous helpings of ridicule are heaped in equal measure on today's polluters and politicians.

But there's also clear recognition that it's no good just blaming someone else. Each and every one of us shares both in the mistakes of the past,and the somewhat more optimistic prospects for the future. That new sense of personal responsibility is what underpins today's increasingly influential Green Movement.

At long last, we seem to be coming to terms with the fact that humankind does not stand apart from the rest of creation. We are inextricably wrapped up in it, and totally dependent on the Earth's life-support systems for our well-being and survival.

The Greek goddess for the Earth was called 'Gaia', and the ancient Greeks took it as a matter of course that they had to nurture and sustain Mother Earth. Slowly and very painfully, we are rediscovering that simple but all-important wisdom.

Hence my own puny contribution to this collection of limericks!

The human dilemma would seem to be dire:
Pollution; destitution; the forests on fire.
But we mustn't despair,
The solutions are there,
If we learn to live as guardians of Gaia.

Jonathon Porritt
Director of Friends of the Earth

The Publishers gratefully acknowledge the kind permission of the authors to reproduce the limericks in this collection. The Publishers would also like to thank the celebrities and the MPs who provided their material at such short notice.

AGE GROUP: 5-11

1st Prize

There was a young leaflet from Crewe
From Margaret's party – quite blue.
But then he was seen
Converted to Green
As a recycled roll in the loo.

Jonathan Bradfield (11)

Runner Up

There was an old man from Devizes
Who grew marrows of prize-winning sizes
But the chemical feed
That achieved this growth speed
Caused local environment crises.

Jacob McClure (11)

AGE GROUP: 12 – 16

1st Prize

When a neutron meets friendly uranium
They react, safely sealed in titanium.
The power you don't mind,
But the waste left behind,
Could zap half the cells in your cranium.

Emma Schofield (16)

Runner Up

There was a young Green of North Denby
Who knew friends of the earth were so trendy,
That everything green
Was so fresh and so clean
That he fell for a lettuce named Wendy.

Helen Davies (13)

AGE GROUP: 17 upwards

1st Prize

Off Blackpool the smaller crustaceans
Are suff'ring from nasty mutations,
When plucked from the sea
They're not he or she
But both, due to Man's aberrations.

C. Rycroft

Runner Up

Oh, Maggie, how we shall miss you
Too late, you espoused the Green issue,
The hole in the sky
Brings a tear to your eye
Which you wipe with a bleached paper tissue.

Mrs Pat Faircloth

Highly Commended

From the tip of my tail to my nose,
The softest of fluffy hair grows,
In fact I'm a gerbil
But prior to Chernobyl,
I worked as a waiter at Joe's.

Brian P. Jones

Highly Commended

The Environment Minister Ridley
Thinks Public Enquiries too fiddly.
'The whole concept's obscene!
Do they think I am green?
Tiddily, widdily, widdily!'

Robin Bateman

In the 40's he studied theology;
In the 50's was tuned into psychology;
In the 60's a Mod;
In the 70's just odd;
Now, a gard'ner, he's into ecology.

F.G. Robinson

Too long has this Earth of ours been
A dispiriting, desolate scene.
Please, let's not destroy it,
But live to enjoy it
By switching all systems to Green!

Alan Clark

I would award the nobel prize,
To the person who cleans up the skies,
And the earth and the sea
As spotless as can be,
Let's hope the world really tries.

Hilary Feinmann (11)

A couple called Adam and Eve
Decided they wished to conceive.
Their fecund potential
Made growth exponential
And left a sick planet to grieve.

Jeanne Smith

Said the Devil with terrible mirth
'They've made a great mess of the Earth.
They kept cashing in
On original sin
Now it's mine, for the little it's worth.'

Joyce Dunbar

'Goodbye,' cried an oil-covered gannet,
'Oh God, what's become of your planet?'
Said the Lord, 'It's a mess,
And I have to confess
Man has made me regret I began it.'

Brian E. Wood

A conservationist curate from Kew
Got his flock hooked on Genesis Two,
But they weren't very keen
When the church magazine
Got recycled and used in the loo.

Mrs Diana Webb

A professor of (green) anthropology
Was converted to cannibal ontology.
'Recycling!' he cried,
As he juicily fried,
'It's the answer for global ecology!'

Mary Franklin

'I'm into recycling' said Fred,
'Or the planet we live on is dead.
Glass, paper and tin
Never go in my bin
But go round in circles instead.'

Jackie Hinden

An old trawler man from Fastnet
Took his vessel away to Tibet.
He said, 'I'm surmising
If the sea keeps on rising
I'll be doing my fishing here yet.'

Joe Houlihan

A young business farmer from Slough
Developed a methane-free cow
By catalytically converting
The gas it was splurting
To power his rotary plough.

Keith Atherton

Sang a bird on a branch in a tree,
To a dolphin at play in the sea,
'Why can't it be seen,
That if people turned Green,
They might all be as happy as we?'

Sarah Pym

A river of perfect azure
To its banks many people did lure.
There they built a big city
And more's the pity,
Now they live on the banks of a sewer.

Patrick Kelly

There once was a grumpy old man
Who puffed out exhaust from his van,
He killed the bees,
And ruined the trees,
Away from him all animals ran.

Beth Worsley (11)

There was a marine from Eastleigh
Obsessed with the oil in the sea.
He swam up to a slick
Grabbed two seals double quick,
Then revived them with rum on the quay.

Susan J. Higgison

There was a young mole called Fast Fred,
Who tragically now is quite dead,
On the motorway verge,
The moles sange a dirge
For poor Fred, dead because of lead.

R.H. Tyler

I once thought it really inane,
To ask, 'What does petrol contain?'
But now, like the rest
I'm almost obsessed,
We're all getting lead on the brain!

R. Woodhouse

There were two little green men from Mars,
Who studied our gases from cars.
'A hole will arise,'
They said, 'in the skies,
We're glad it's your world and not ours.'

Katherine Handley

There was a Green lady of Stanwick
Who married a motor mechanic.
When asked, 'How could this be?'
Said, 'He's wholly lead-free,
Our attraction is purely organic.'

Sue Thompson

There was a young yuppie from Ware
Who sneered at the Greens with long hair.
With his Porsche on the road
He was like Mr Toad
Till he choked on the lead in the air.

Sue Appleton

Civilized man is so greedy and vain,
He's oblivious to actions insane.
He just thinks he can take
Larger slices of cake,
Will he never for Earth's sake refrain?

Daisy O'Connor

Today we've achieved a finesse
In packaging goods to excess;
Using mountains of plastic,
Foam, nylon – fantastic –
Tomorrow we'll clean up the mess.

Mrs Ruth Blandford

When old Scrooge in the coffin was laid
His young widow remained undismayed.
'With his miserly touch
He would never buy much–
But at least he will bio-degrade . . .'

Miss P.R. Bowring

It's easy to see man doesn't care
About destroying his land, sea and air,
But it's quite supposable
That being decomposable
When he does he'll no longer be there.

Nicholas Winter

There once lived a foolhardy race
In a faraway corner of space;
Blind to its worth,
They poisoned their Earth,
And all disappeared without trace.

Ronald Rubin

There was an old grocer's fair daughter,
Who did all the things that he taught her.
She'd sell any utility,
But it looks like futility
To sell us undrinkable water.

P.J. Powles

The Rev. Brown, a cuckolded vicar
Became suicidal – his life couldn't get sicker.
But which method to choose
Gas, electricity, noose
Or tap water – which his wife said was quicker!

Gaythorne Sylvester

There was a smart yuppie called Porter
Who hated to pay for his water.
Moaned he, 'When I pee,
It's recyled, you see;
I don't get a yield, but I oughta.'

Charles Brien

Said the seal to the salmon and otters,
'Did God really design us as blotters,
To mop up the oil
From the sea and the soil
Spewed out by those corporate rotters?'

W.B. Crouch

There once was a planet so fair,
With safe soil, pure water, clean air.
Then mankind arrived
And quickly contrived
To poison the lot everywhere.

Miss D. Elthorne-Jones

An MP from East Aberdeen
Believed that our coastline was clean,
Until came the day
He swam in a bay,
And my, did the fellow turn green!

Bernard Clarke

Is the beach still a nice place to play?
Do you fancy a swim in the bay?
Then make sure you don't sink,
Or you might have to drink
What you passed on the previous day!

Mrs L.F. Ménage

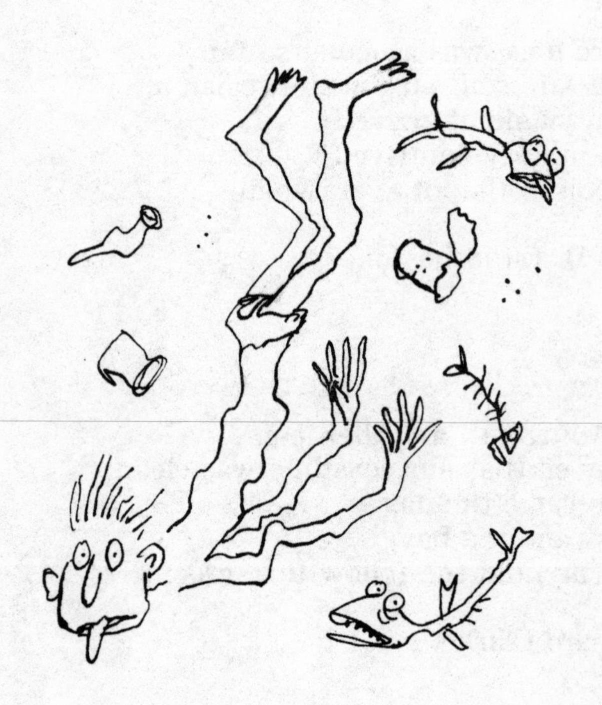

To clean up the earth we must try,
We can start by cleaning the sky
Then clean up the sea
The meadow, the lea,
And say what a good boy am I!

Spike Milligan

I am a friend of the earth
The place where I had my birth.
I won't chop trees down
Or let animals drown
Without them, what would life be worth?

Thomas Conolly (8)

There was a young lady from Sheen
Whose outlook was starting to green,
While planting a tree
She was stung by a bee
Now on sit-ins she isn't so keen!

Maureen Lenk

As aliens passed in their craft,
They saw a blue planet and laughed:
'I think it's called ''Earth'',
Give it a wide berth,
It stinks, and its people are daft.'

Tim Waits (13)

A little green man from Outer Space
Came to earth with a frown on his face,
He said, 'Will you stop spraying,
For the ozone's decaying
And we don't want your junk in our place.'

Kate Ashton (8)

There was a young Green of Dunoon,
Who said, 'If we don't do something soon,
To preserve all the niches
And conserve the species,
The earth will end up like the moon.'

Viv Doyle

Said the voice on the heavenly mike,
'I'm God, and I know what I like:
The planet unheated,
The ozone repleted,
And President, David Icke.'

Sam Leithiton

To clean up the world from pollution
Will require a quite drastic solution,
So prove your own worth
Join Friends of the Earth
And be part of the Green revolution.

Caroline Windsor

The political colouring-book
Has suddenly got a new look;
They're all awfully keen
To be seen to be 'green' –
How simple, yet *how* long it took!

Miss P.R. Bowring

An ostrich from a tropical land
Once buried his head in the sand.
The move was a riot,
They all had to try it –
Evading the issue was grand!

Aileen Hunter

Said Thatcher, 'I want to be seen
As anti-pollution and clean,
So I'm changing my hue
From Conservative Blue
To radiant Nuclear Green!'

Mrs. N.V. Lyne

'We are Green,' cried the grandmother turning,
Carboniferous combustions spurning,
'The Greenhouse Effect
Shall be instantly checked
For the lady is not for burning.'

Mr P.F. Hughes

To the P.M.'s intense irritation
Greens demanded, without 'quivocation,
That she concede how at birth
Man inherits the Earth,
Not a miserable scrap called 'My Nation'.

Anthony Hentschel

The Minister spoke with authority
With weighty and ringing sonority,
'Clean the rivers,' he said,
'Save the seals and ban lead,
Conserve my imperilled majority!'

S. Williams

The Environment Minister felt
That a blow to the Greens should be dealt.
So he poisoned the water
Removed what they'd fought for,
Then hit them below the Green Belt.

Ian Frances

An Archbishop living in Kent
Deplored how the wild flowers went.
He pronounced – through the media –
'We prefer our fields weedier.
Will you please give up Paraquat for Lent.'

J. Macnaughton

Said a brave Young Conservative, Frank,
After fretting all day at the Bank:
'I'll stop using these
Under-arm CFC's.'
So he went on as normal, and stank.

Glyn Maxwell

There once was a husband called Denis,
Who said, 'Holes at the Poles are a menace,
Maggie dear, please
Outlaw CFC's,
So the only city on water is Venice.'

Simon Oliver

Mrs Thatcher said, 'No one is Greener,
Or environmentally keener,
Ozone holes we must mend,
The rainforests defend
And perhaps we'll recycle Edwina!'

Mrs C. Lawton

A graffiti artist, living in Utrecht
Was concerned by the Greenhouse Effect.
Writing 'Kilroy was here'
It soon became clear
That a 'roll on' is hard to detect.

Mark McCarthy

At which college d'you think they will be
Our grandsons in 2040?
Let us heed the warning
Of global warming
Or we may find it's Salford-on-Sea!

Richard Hughes

Said Maggie to Denis one day,
'The planet is melting away.
Perhaps we should switch
From moving to Dulwich
And retire to the Milky Way.'

Guy Williams

We should care for the earth's varied terrain,
The forest, the river, the plain,
From Andes to Eiger
Savannah to Taiga,
And cherish the life they sustain.

Paul Rand

There once was a planet called Earth,
Which gave every life-form its birth,
One called Man, in its greed,
Took far more than its need
So died out, never knowing its worth.

J. Swann

Oh why does nobody mind?
Why are we cruel and so blind
To the state of the seas
And the fate of the trees,
How come we are labelled mankind?

Mrs B. Myers

A gent at Waterloo Station
Created quite a sensation;
He stood on box
In brilliant green socks
And lectured on conservation.

Pauline C.E. Harris

There was a young Green of Dundee
Who made his home in a tree.
His needs were quite few
And to the Earth he felt true,
For he was closer to nature you see.

Bridget Icke

There was a young Green of Djibouti
Who felt it was really her duty
To give up hair spray
And throw it away,
Thus putting Earth before beauty.

Marcia Melville-Ross

There was a young lady called Packer
Who never used hairspray or lacquer.
Tho' her hair was like wire
She did not desire
That layer of ozone to knacker.

Victoria Wood

A friendly old layer called Ozone
Stopped the Earth getting too Hot or Frozone
But the folks who enjoyed it
Were reckless, destroyed it,
Now where there was Ozone, there's Nozone.

Simon Killingworth

There's a CFC in my spray
And I use it every day.
The Greens get uptight
But I am all right,
For it's my children who'll pay.

S. Phillips

We live in a world with a dearth
Of folk who acknowledge its worth;
It's a jewel in space
But will die without trace
Unless we're *all* friends of this Earth.

Mrs L. Rogers

In fifty years' time I declare,
Because of this Greenhouse affair,
We'll spend our vacations
At seaside locations
Like Bradford or Slough-Super-Mare.

Mr J. Fielding

Come yuppies, beware global warming,
The melting of ice caps is dawning.
When your dock penthouse flat
Becomes seal habitat,
You will wish you had heeded our warning.

Ms. M. Makepeace

A mouth-organ player from Utrecht
Was alarmed by the Greenhouse Effect.
In order to reduce CO_2
He sucked more than he blew
Till his health – and his organ – were wrecked.

Harold Olorenshaw

There is a large hole in the sky
Whose profile is terribly high.
So now it's quite trendy
To buy ozone-friendly,
And lo, the end is not nigh!

David Bartlett

A hair-dresser I know but won't name,
Is just not playing the game,
I saw the wrong spray
In his salon today
He should be crawling with shame.

Pauline C.E. Harris

Frank Bruno (The Fighting Machine)
Said to Harry, 'I want to be Green.
I'll fight CFC's
And plant lots of trees.
Eh Harry, y'know what I mean?'

Kevin Godby

There once was a colour called green
That politicians would never have been.
But now for the heck of it
(Or to woo the electorate)
They all must be seen to be green.

Mr K. Tubby

A pearl-bedecked lady from Grantham
Has just changed her political anthem –
'Rejoice in the trees,
The birds and the bees.'
Clearly she'll now privatise them!

James Corr

There was a grandmother of true blue
Who recently altered her hue.
Now she'll stop all pollution
By funding the solution –
Believe that? You're green if you do.

Gordon Scott

There once was a lady Prime Minister
Who said that her aims were not sinister.
She said that she's Green,
Environmentally clean,
But I think she is more *eau de nihilister*.

Mrs P.A. Morgan

When politicians say they are 'green',
One wonders what they really mean,
For all their hot air
Only rises to share
In the Greenhouse Effect it would seem!

Richard Raymond-Barker

The lady U-turned and was keen
To exude an impression of green,
So she waved like the trees
And roared like the seas,
Sincere as the rivers are clean.

Meurig Jones

Said a certain grandmother called Thatcher,
'On the world stage we're someone of stature,
And methinks we detect
In the Greenhouse Effect
A disaster-to-visit vote-catcher.'

Henry Clements

It was said that ‘An apple a day
Will best keep the doctor away.’
But now one can’t eat it
Since growers maltreat it
And squirt it with chemical spray.

Elizabeth Satterthwaite

There once was an organic sprout
That was additive-free without doubt.
But wasn’t it tragic
All that muck and magic
Got served with a luminous trout?

Claire Collison

There once was a farmer called Rand
Who sprayed pesticide over his land,
And all that he said
When people fell dead
Was, ‘I’ll use it until it is banned.’

Ian Stuart

The loss of each rainforest tree
May lead to a rise in the sea.
So let's ponder before
We select a new door
And choose softwood or UPVC.

Peter Burns

A Power Station quite near our farm
Had an accident causing 'No Harm'.
So there's no need to panic
All that's green is organic
And my leg is as long as my arm!

Patricia Thirgood

There was a young man from St Ives
Who sprayed chemicals over his chives.
The plants felt abused
By the toxins he used
And the mixture corroded his knives.

Caroline Jenkins

There was a young organic farmer
Who really was rather a charmer,
He kept fat, happy hens,
And lovely pig-pens,
And even a free-range llama.

B. Trounce

The virtues of lentil and bean
By all parties now have been seen.
Deep blue and deep red
Have no wish to be dead,
So they're all fighting hard to be green.

Gillian Hogg

An organic young gardener from Sale
Collected his slugs in a pail.
'I hate pesticide,
It's immoral!' he cried,
Before drowning the buggers in ale.

David Mather

A wildlife gardener named Reg
Grew a haven of meadow and hedge.
The birds ate the bugs
And the frogs ate the slugs
And Reg ate the organic veg.

Mrs C.A. Jones

An ecologist chappie said, 'Why
Must I keep my backyard very spry?
I'll have weeds, reeds and bogs,
Nettles, slugs, bats and frogs
And I'll call it an S.S.S.I.'

Mrs June Crew

A prince of the world had a need
To speak to the plant and the weed.
He did all in his power
So the planet could flower,
While his thoughts were scattered like seed.

John Watkins

The carcinogen sun no one cares to brave,
All fossil fuels no one bothers to save,
There's no reason to care
No more blind frightened stare,
For here we lie in our untended grave.

John Wildgoose

On the pollution-free beach at Cromer
A sunbather turned over and over;
His tan and his swimming
Attracted the women
And also a small melanoma.

Lee Gannon

A foolish young fellow named Mark
Swam off Sellafield once, for a lark.
Now his becquerel* level
Has gone to the devil
And he glows for miles in the dark.

John Colmans

* Unit of measure of nuclear radiation

An agricultural spokesman of wit
When asked if he thought it was fit
To irradiate food
Said, 'Don't think I'm rude –
It's the only way folk'll eat shit.'

Terry Jones

A prophet of doom from Utrecht
Predicted the Greenhouse Effect.
He said, 'When we are drowned,
With a seaweed surround,
You'll have to admit I'm correct.'

Mr J. Fielding

A consumer who consumed all he could
Said, 'I'd be Green if only they would
Enliven the choice
And make my Rolls Royce
Out of bio-degradable wood.'

Jane Bell

There was a young Green from Bordeaux
Whose body was all of a-glow:
But it wasn't the wine
That made his cheeks shine,
It was holes in the ozone you know.

Alan Copperwheat

The wards and museums were shutting,
The backers were beaming and strutting;
The air was a fog
The Thames was a bog,
And the 'Garden of England' a cutting.

Glyn Maxwell

A vandal whom sunstroke drove manic
Gave up CFC's in a panic.
His art stayed obscene,
But his slogans turned Green,
And now his graffiti's organic.

Mrs N. Bevan

A greengrocer whose goods were select
Supplied fruit to the priesthood elect.
'Is this,' said the nuns,
Seeing the size of his plums,
'What they mean by the Greenhouse Effect?'

Steve Stafford

A man with a chemical spray
Came drenching the orchard today.
The death of the bee
Will sting you and me–
Speak up for the Earth while you may.

Miss P.R. Bowring

There lived a brave man in Brazil
'Till greed marked him down for the kill.
Until his life ended
The trees he defended,
Now, Mendes, your name lives on still.

Iris Ivinson

They are chopping the rainforest down,
To make way for another new town,
Creatures are crying,
The plants are dying,
Mother Nature looks on with a frown.

Jennifer Howliston (11)

'Timber!' cried the man with the saw
As the tree fell down to the floor
And on him, defenceless,
Knocking him senseless,
He doesn't chop trees any more.

Nigel Caroll

There was a young man from Brazil
Who cut down the trees on a hill.
It rained all one day
And the soil washed away
So life on the hill is now nil.

Colin Nicholls

An aspiring young actor, James Dean,
Caused a stir in Macbeth's final scene.
When the trees came from Birnam
He marched up and told 'em
To go back to where they had been.

Diana Webb

A fussy young woman of Leigh
Said, 'Woodman, do please spare that tree.
It lies at the edge
Of my back garden hedge,
And my dog likes to sit there and admire the sunset

Dr Patrick Moore CBE FRAS

A rainforest was owned by a Brazilian
Whose trees numbered well over a million.
That man, the great clot,
He hacked down the lot
And beef-burgered himself into oblivion.

Stuart Morris

The world's the green tree that we land on,
The tree's the green life which we hand on,
And the sawing you hear
Is polluters, my dear,
At work on the branch that we stand on.

Stephen Sylvester

The trees in the forests are dying,
But nobody seems to be crying.
Acid rain is to blame
It's a disgusting shame
With governments and companies all lying.

Janice White

Said the monkey, 'Man's taught me to see,
That the jungle's no place for my tree.
It was clearly created
To be chopped down and grated
For pulp to write books about me.'

Anthony Cheke

In politics there's now a dearth
Of proposals with any great worth,
But in terms of survival
The Greens have no rival –
Their aim is to save Planet Earth.

Gundula Dorey

An inspector as thick as two planks
Thought all FOE supporters were cranks.
He said 'I agree
With the CEGB –.
Accept Hinkley C and say thanks!'

Carole Kyhlmann

There was an old man of Thorpeness
Who gazed on the world in distress,
He could see Sizewell B,
Seals dying at sea
And beaches an oily mess.

D. Head

There was an old lady from Hale
Who thought she would help save the whale,
She put one in her bath,
But much to her wrath,
She was killed with a flick of its tail.

Mrs A. Rennie

There was a young lady in Dover,
Who loved verges all filled with white clover.
But on one dreadful day
They were poisoned with spray,
Now the clover in Dover is over.

Mrs. D.O. Thompson

A nursery gardener called Henshall
Thought chemical feeds inessential.
On his land he replaced
Them with recycled waste
And enhanced his productive potential.

Martin Forrest

A blue politician was keen
To join the ecology scene,
So she posed for the press
In a bright yellow dress–
And came out a delicate green.

Roy Dean

The woman in charge of this nation
Has just learnt to spell 'conservation'.
But with nuclear trains
And the rivers like drains,
Market forces spell early damnation.

Colin Alston

A formidable Tory named Thatcher
Thought on Green issues none could match her,
Till one day, on a whim
In the sea she did swim
And ten million bacilli dispatched her.

Sandra Raftery

A blue whale was heard to keen,
'My goodness, I have gone green!'
'You're not alone,'
The pink turtle did groan,
'There's Thatcher, the Pope and the Queen.'

Patrick O'Neill

Green issues caused many a quarrel
Till the Greening of Britain went Royal;
Said the Queen, 'I shall be
CFC and lead free!'
Will there be bottle banks at Balmoral?

Catherine Simmons

There was a young fellow called Porritt,
Who knew a good cause when he saw it,
So he spread the Green word
Until everyone heard,
And now we *all* say we are for it!

William Waldegrave, MP

He laughed all the way to the bank
With a barrel of poison that stank,
But a swimmer downstream
Gave an agonised scream,
Turned purple all over and sank!

Richard Blomfield

A girl with a problem was faced
Rushed off to her doctor in haste.
He said with a laugh
As she broke in half,
'My dear, you've got toxic waist!'

David Blackburn

Whenever a young man called Cooper
Saw a 'whoopsie', he'd swear like a trooper.
He would say, 'The solution
To dogs' pavement polution
Is to pick up the poop with a scooper.'

Bob Halliwell

Felicity Yuppy from Knowle,
Took home a bright pink toilet roll.
Tarquin said, 'That won't do,
Only *white* in our loo,
Dear girl, the World's on parole!'

Mrs Susan Hudson

Up there in the clouds, all defiant,
Was our Jack and the beanstalk giant!
Says Jack, 'It's a pain!
For this damned acid rain
Has made my escape unreliant!'

Mark Abraham

The pollution came out in masses,
A whole load of horrible gases,
They floated up high,
Far into the sky,
Now acid falls when a cloud passes.

Ian Bamford (11)

There once were some people in Wick
Who were radioactively sick.
When Nirex got it wrong
They didn't last long–
But there *once* were some people in Wick.

Mrs E. M. Buchanan

A cautious young chap making tea,
Boiled some Perrier, explaining: 'You see,
It's not H_2O
That's been worrying me so
But the Pb and 245T.'

Julia Noyes

A spokesman for BNFL
Was explaining how all would be well,
Should a pressure flask fail
Or a night train derail–
Just ring up your broker and sell.

Janet James

My hopes for this planet have faded,
By ozone we're no longer shaded,
If the Greenhouse Effect
Does what they expect,
We'll soon all be bio-degraded!

M. Creer

A holiday walk in the Lakes
Demands from the heart what it takes.
But a Chernobyl gust
Transforms dew into dust,
And the sight of dead sheep nauseates.

John Hawkins

Said a young Cumbrian Green to his mam,
'I fancy a nice bit o' lamb.'
Said his mother, 'Nay lad,
T'radiation's so bad
You'd be far better off wi' tinned spam.'

Agnes Crayston

There was a young green from Dumfries
Who worried about CFC's.
He said, 'I object
To the Greenhouse Effect
Which is heating us up by degrees.'

Angela James

There was a young man of Nantucket
Who went to a well with a bucket.
The well had run dry
So he tried not to cry,
And sat himself down and said . . . 'Bother!'

Geoffrey Lean

There once was a planet called Earth
Which began to decline at Man's birth,
For he took for his needs
What were really his greeds
And plundered for all he was worth.

Diane Burgess

A tumble in hay, I oft yearn
But not when yon stubble's aburn,
For the heat of desire
Can quickly expire
As the flames of the field draw astern.

A. Sunderland

Yesterday while eating a snack
I was seized with a guilt attack –
Forests are razed
And cattle grazed
To end up in a Big Mac.

Jeff Gerecke

In the next fifty years while we sink
Perhaps we will all learn to think
Of the sprays, CFC's
And the saving of trees
As not just some 'Lefty Green' kink.

Daniel Tobias

There was a Green lass from Arbroath
Who remarked on the subject of growth,
'We can either have quality
Of life in our polity,
Or volume of goods – but not both.'

Tony Beamish

The new aerosol spray that we buy
Can make terrible holes in the sky,
So read every label
And we should be able
To lead better lives if we try.

Charles Romito (8)

One day when the petrol runs out
And the last tiny drop leaves the spout,
I'll go where I like
On my trusty old bike
Saying, 'How nice with no traffic about.'

Charlotte Lewis (11)

There once was a leopard with spots
Who thought he'd prefer stripes to his dots.
He washed them away
It took him all day,
But still he's dodging the hunters' shots.

Louise Purnell (12)

There were woods where I played as a child:
Ponds with tadpoles and all creatures wild.
Now it's bricks, dirt and smell,
Cry out, 'Stop those who sell
Our birthright, and leave us defiled!'

Miss F. Waite

A minister named Mr Ridley
Said, 'Green Belt legislation is fiddly.
I'll give no further thought
To problems I ought,
Just fill it all up, very quickly!'

Peter Strange

There once was an Environment Minister,
Who thought everything green must be sinister.
'On fifty cigs a day,
I do intend to stay
Until the last rites they administer.'

David Bexon

I'm told that the story is true
Why the Tories are changing their hue:
The cowards are yellow
So ask any fellow –
To make green you just mix it with blue.

Gareth Hughes

While waiting for sense to prevail
Over ozone, rainforest and whale,
For this planet's release
We pray that Greenpeace
And Friends of the Earth do not fail!

Graham Wilkinson

A planet named Earth was designed
With the well-being of creatures in mind.
Created in green
It was rendered obscene
By the lifestyle of modern mankind.

Mr P. D. Ridge

There was a young fellow called Ted,
Who had voted Blue, Yellow and Red,
But when he had seen
The wisdom of Green
He slept much more easily in bed.

G.A. Lee

Let's see if I've got this correct:
When all politicians elect
To care about trees
And debate CFC's
It's known as the 'Green House' effect.

Bob Picheral

There was a young lady of Perth
Who regarded the Greens with much mirth.
Then she heard of the hole
In ozone at the Pole
And now she's a Friend of the Earth.

Frank Dunstan

There was a shrewd Green from Ealing
Who grew fruit and veg on the ceiling,
He said, 'I suspect
It's the Greenhouse Effect
But now I can weed without kneeling.'

S.P. Lucas

There was a Green lady from Leeds
Who swallowed a packet of seeds.
Now out of her nose
Grows a rambling rose
And she gets greenfly all over her tweeds.

David Orchard

A Friend of the Earth named Amanda
Admitted with praiseworthy candour
That her contribution
To water distribution
Was sharing her bath with a panda.

Mrs Mary Wilson

The future of every planet
Depends on the people who man it;
If they're driven by greed
And not by their need,
It'll soon be a dead lump of granite.

James Wiegold

There was a Prime Minister who
In a quandary knew not what to do,
Until with adroit alacrity
Regained some popularity
Metamorphosing to green from blue.

J.L. Nichols

Now that everyone's frightfully keen,
To be viewed as the darkest-hued 'Green',
We'll have to ensure
(It's a natural law)
That their wallet is where their mouth's been.

Chris Patten, MP

Said a woman about to give birth,
'Put his name down for Friends of the Earth.
He must learn to think Green,
Keep the waterways clean
And know what the ozone is worth.'

Marie Higbee

A wise old ruler of ours
Gazed, through the Hole, at the stars:
He thought of The Vast
And Russians hurtling past
And said, 'Let's put people on Mars.'

Ken Bingham

An astronaut high in the sky,
Looked down on the Earth with sigh.
He wept for the lost trees
And fish dead in the seas,
And waved the old planet goodbye.

Jackie Murphy

In the rivers our poison is flowing,
In the jungles our fires are glowing.
Should God recreate
Earth's primeval state
Would man get a chance on this showing?

Mr R. O. Jones

The profligate species of man
Reproduced till the Earth overran.
He wasted resources,
Defied Nature's forces,
Then tried to stop just what he began.

Jill Nevile

At this time in our creation
There is over-population.
To keep families small
Is not hard at all,
Just cut down on copulation.

Spike Milligan

No doubt once this great contest ends
You'll pulp all the forms like good friends,
And doubtless old Spike'll
Quite gladly recycle
The verses that everyone sends!

Bernard Clarke

'The Earth has been quite a success,'
Said God, 'but I have to confess
The creation of Man
Rather buggered the plan
For he makes such a terrible mess.'

Philip Bird

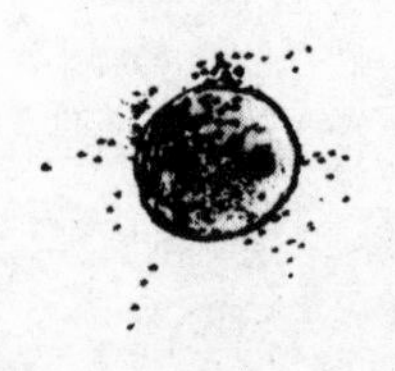

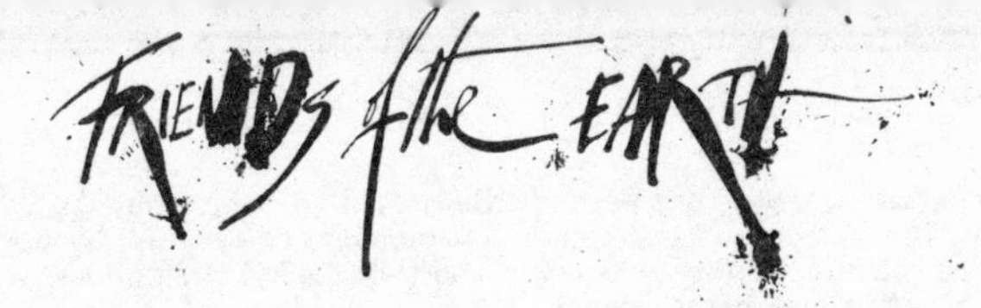

WHO ARE THE FRIENDS OF THE EARTH?

Friends of the Earth is one of the leading environmental pressure groups in the UK. We blow the whistle on those who destroy the environment, and we put pressure on those who have the power to protect it. We represent the concerns and interests of many thousands of people. Through lobbying and effective PR, we can make their voice heard in the corridors of power, the boardrooms of industry and every household in the land.

NATIONALLY

Backed by more than 100,000 supporters, Friends of the Earth campaigns on a dozen major issues. We commission detailed research to underpin these campaigns, and provide extensive information materials to enable everyone to do their bit for the environment.

We work with *all* political parties, but are aligned to none. Our effectiveness depends on our political impartiality, and we have built up an impressive reputation for giving 'early warnings' of environmental hazards – on acid rain, pesticides, the ozone layer and the 'Greenhouse Effect'. But politicians rarely act until public pressure forces them to. Friends of the Earth exists to mobilise that pressure for change.

LOCALLY

Friends of the Earth has a network of more than 270 Local Groups across the country. It was the threat of a coordinated boycott of ozone-damaging aerosols by these groups which persuaded the aerosol industry to phase out the use of CFCs as propellants by the end of 1989.

We also coordinate more than 50 Earth Action groups, involving young people between the ages of 14 and 23.

INTERNATIONALLY

Friends of the Earth International is now represented in more than 35 countries with groups in Brazil and Malaysia; in Poland and Estonia; in the US, Canada, Japan and throughout Europe. Our International Secretariat is based here at Underwood Street.

THE CAMPAIGNS

THE OZONE LAYER

Protecting the ozone layer was high on our list of priorities back in the mid-seventies, but it wasn't until 1987 that politicians stopped calling us scare-mongers! Since then, our consumer campaigns against the use of ozone-eating chemicals (CFCs) in aerosols and foam packaging have been enormously successful.

We are now hard at work seeking to eliminate the use of CFCs in insulation materials, refrigeration and microelectronics.

TROPICAL RAINFORESTS

The loss of the world's remaining rainforests is the greatest threat to the global environment today. In 1988 alone, 50,000 square miles of the Brazilian rainforest were razed to the ground by cattle-ranchers and settlers desperately seeking new land. Thousands more acres were destroyed by logging companies and inappropriate industrial development, often funded with money from the World Bank and other Western banks.

Our Rainforest Campaign deals with *all* aspects of this crisis including trade and aid questions and international debt. Within months of publishing our "Good Wood Guide", 100 companies agreed to stop using tropical hardwoods unless they came from properly managed forests.

ACID RAIN

Not so very long ago, few people had even heard of acid rain. In 1983, Friends of the Earth was the first organisation to start campaigning on this issue, highlighting the appalling threat to our forests, lakes, rivers and buildings. We have seen some progress on reducing emissions from power stations, but the UK Government continues to resist tough measures to reduce pollution from cars and lorries.

ENERGY

The nuclear industry is in decline. Its contribution to our energy needs (2%) is still tiny. It is uneconomic, unsafe and unnecessary. The human costs of Chernobyl will be paid in terms of many thousands of additional cancer deaths throughout Europe over the next 20 or 30 years. Our evidence to the Sizewell and Hinkley Point Public Inquiries has helped to sway public opinion against this continuing absurdity.

GLOBAL WARMING

For all these reasons, nuclear power can provide absolutely no answer to the problem of "The Greenhouse Effect" – the gradual warming of the atmosphere caused by the release of carbon dioxide and other "greenhouse gases".

By contrast, we have consistently promoted a policy based on energy conservation, increased efficiency, the cleaner use of our remaining fossil fuels, and the long-term development of renewable energy sources such as wind, wave, solar and tidal power.

CITIES FOR PEOPLE

Our cities are now paying the price for years of insensitive planning, environmental neglect and the total dominance of the motor car in transport policy.

Friends of the Earth campaigns actively for the rights of cyclists, pedestrians and all users of public transport. We work closely with local authorities to promote an integrated approach to the urban environment, and are heavily involved in protecting "green spaces" within our cities and reducing pollution on our streets.

COUNTRYSIDE AND AGRICULTURE

The Government's Wildlife and Countryside Act has totally failed to provide adequate protection for Britain's countryside. Modern farming techniques have caused grave damage to the wider countryside, and we have been in the forefront of the campaign to promote sustainable, environmentally-sensitive alterntives, including organic farming.

Our Pesticides Campaign, launched in 1984, forced the government to introduce tighter controls on pesticide use through the Food and Environment Protection Act. Since then, we have continued to highlight the problems of aerial spraying and pesticide residues in both food and water.

RECYLING AND UK2000

Friends of the Earth first hit the headlines in 1971 by dumping thousands of non-returnable bottles on the doorstep of Schweppes! Since that time, we have actively promoted many different measures to encourage the recycling of glass, paper, aluminium and plastics, as well as putting direct pressure on industry and retailers to reduce today's appallingly wasteful packaging.

Through the Government's UK2000 initiative, Friends of the Earth has also been able to set up and support grass-roots recycling schemes.

WATER POLLUTION

The water we drink is at risk from many pollutants, particularly pesticides, nitrates, aluminium and lead. The Government has repeatedly breached the EEC's Directive on Drinking Water, and only formal complaints from Friends of the Earth to the European Commission have forced the Water Authorities to start cleaning up their act. It is the polluters of our rivers and water supplies who should be made to pay the full cost of cleaning them up – *not* the consumer.

TOXIC WASTES

In 1988, when the Karin B threatened to offload its toxic cargo in the UK, we created such a storm of protest that the Department of the Environment had no option but to send it packing.

The whole waste managements system is in a mess. Both the Waste Disposal Authorities and the Pollution Inspectorate are hopelessly under-resourced. Friends of the Earth is campaigning for a rigorous new licensing and regulatory system, and for a complete ban on the import of wastes for land-fill in the UK.

If you would like more information about the work of Friends of the Earth, or would like details about membership, please telephone 01-490 4734

50 things you can do to save the Earth

1. Plant a tree.
2. Change the light bulbs to energy efficient types. Modern bulbs are 80% more efficient. Each bulb you change will save the equivalent energy of four sacks of coal.
3. Use recycled paper loo rolls. In any colour you like. Coloured papers are just as bio-degradable as white.
4. Use only CFC free aerosols.
5. Support population control programmes.
6. Change to unleaded petrol.
7. Insulate the loft.
8. Use the bottle banks.
9. Keep to the speed limit. Never drive faster than you have to.
10. Write to your MP on recycled paper and tell him/her how you're watching the record on green issues.
11. Fruit and vegetables don't need to be plastic wrapped. Refuse them if they are.
12. Cycle or walk when possible – don't drive.
13. Use public transport.
14. Have cooler baths and showers.
15. Eat locally produced food. It saves transport costs.
16. Switch to organic food.
17. Use terry nappies.
18. Turn down the thermostat on your central heating boiler.
19. Boycott companies who cut down tropical rain-forests.
20. Don't buy 'disposable' products. They end up producing methane in land fill sites.
21. Fit a gas condensing boiler in your home. 25% more efficient.
22. Check your tyre pressures. Correct inflation saves fuel.
23. Fit radiator thermostats.
24. Avoid diesel.
25. Write to your local newspaper about local pollution.
26. Fight back against tarmac terrorism. Write to Rt. Hon. Cecil

Parkinson M.P., Secretary of State for Transport about the national roads programme.

27. Collect aluminium foil.
28. Insist on milk bottles not one-trip cartons.
29. Give up smoking.
30. When you buy a new fridge insist the retailer takes back your old one and recycles the CFC safely.
31. Clean up the messes your dog makes.
32. Ask your council to install a paper bank along side the bottle bank.
33. Set up a paper recycling scheme in your office.
34. Use rechargeable batteries.
35. Ask for advice on energy saving from Energy Efficiency Office, Dept. of Energy,
    Thames House South, Millbank, London SW1P 4QJ.
36. Buy only energy efficient electrical goods.
37. Find out whether you can fit a catalytic converter to your car.
38. Insist on free range eggs.
39. Use natural cosmetics.
40. Use non-toxic cleaning products and use only as much as you really need.
41. Lobby your council for more green spaces.
42. Save energy. Switch off something.
43. Share your car.
44. Refuse items made from mahogany, ramin, iroko or teak.
45. Control garden pests without petroleum-based pesticides.
46. Consider vegetarianism. It's more energy efficient.
47. Don't eat burgers from boxes containing CFCs.
48. Use cardboard boxes not supermarket plastic bags.
49. Wear natural fibres.
50. Join Friends of the Earth,
    26-28 Underwood Street,
    London N1 7JQ
    Tel: 01-490 1555

Produced by Ogilvy & Mather Advertising. **Friends of the Earth**